100

THINGS TO DO IN

SAVANNAH

BEFORE YOU

DIE

100
THINGS TO DO IN
SAVANNAH
BEFORE YOU
DIE

• •

ZACH POWERS

REEDY PRESS

Library of Congress Control Number: 2016955744

ISBN: 9781681060668

Design by Jill Halpin

Cover photo and all interior photos by Joshua A. Powers unless otherwise noted.
Author cover photo by Stephanie Raines.

Printed in the United States of America
17 18 19 20 21   5 4 3 2 1

Please note that websites, phone numbers, addresses, and company names are subject
to change or cancellation. We did our best to relay the most accurate information
available, but due to circumstances beyond our control, please do not hold us liable for
misinformation. When exploring new destinations, please do your homework before
you go.

DEDICATION

To Gram, one of the first tour bus drivers in Savannah, and Granny, one of Tybee Island's longest-standing residents.

ATLANTA   CHARLESTON   CHICAGO   NEW YORK

FLORIDA   HAWAII   LAS VEGAS   ANGELES   PARIS   WASHINGTON

CONTENTS

• •

• •

Culture and History

• •

• •

• •

PREFACE

Savannah is called the Hostess City of the South, and this book is your personal guide to taking advantage of our hospitality, whether you're new to town or a local looking for a few fresh activities.

The following pages introduce you to 100 reasons Savannah is such a beloved community. The History and Culture section guides you to the must-see sights in the Historic District. Dive into our vibrant art scene, including world-class galleries and museums. Need a nightcap? The Drink section overflows with suggestions. And find dining and shopping options for every mood and budget.

Yes, there are far more than 100 things worth doing in Savannah, so use this book to start exploring all our city has to offer. And keep it handy when you're out and about. You never know when one of its tips might lead you to a new adventure.

While most of the places mentioned in this book are situated within walkable Downtown Savannah, a few—such as Tybee Island and Bonaventure Cemetery—lie farther out and will require transportation. Please confirm details with each establishment before visiting. The information is accurate as of publication, but menus, hours, and prices are subject to change.

—Zach Powers

ACKNOWLEDGMENTS

Savannah is a special place because of the people who choose to live here. I'm grateful to those who have worked at shops or restaurants or bars, the tour guides and hospitality professionals, and everyone else who helps make Downtown Savannah such a vibrant setting. I wrote most of this book sitting in Gallery Espresso, so thanks to the crew there for providing coffee and flat surfaces. Thanks to my colleagues at Telfair Museums for introducing me to the inner working of Savannah's tourism industry. And lastly, thanks to the generations of Powerses and Beechers who have called the Savannah area home.

FOOD AND DRINK

PERK UP
AT SAVANNAH'S OLDEST COFFEE SHOP

Gallery Espresso has served as Savannah's living room for more than twenty years. The coffee shop/art gallery overlooks the stately oaks in historic Chippewa Square and draws an even mix of locals and visitors. In addition to Gallery's titular espresso, you can choose from more than a hundred varieties of loose-leaf teas, cold drinks for hot days, and several brews of drip coffee made fresh from morning to night. For food, Gallery offers a satisfying slate of coffee shop standards, plus luscious desserts and both made-to-order and ready-made sandwiches and wraps. Arrive early on weekend mornings for fresh filled croissants. The Gallery staff welcomes book readers and laptop workers, and coffee refills are always cheap, so don't be shy about lingering. Before you leave, circle the room for a look at the art, with new works from local and regional artists cycling in monthly.

234 Bull St., 912-233-5348
galleryespresso.com

THE HOME OF
SAVANNAH'S BOHEMIANS

Where do all the hippies meet? The Sentient Bean! Not to mention musicians, poets, and performers of all ilks. The Bean, as it's usually called by locals, has served coffee and organic grub in an authentic Bohemian environment for more than fifteen years. Come for the coffee, yes, but make sure you stick around for one of the regular evening shows, which range from spoken word and music open mics to concerts to indie film screenings. Visitors to Forsyth Park also make the Bean their preferred refreshment stop. The front door is just across the street at the park's south end. So stop by after a stroll and grab a coffee. They even offer organic beer and wine. And check the big calendar on the back wall to find an upcoming event.

13 E. Park Ave., 912-232-4447
sentientbean.com

A CUP OF JOE
WHEREVER YOU GO

For years, Savannah was limited to only two independent coffee shops, but that number has exploded over the past several years. Foxy Loxy anchors the south end of Downtown and whips up a delicious assortment of tacos as well as coffee sourced from local roaster PERC. Occupying two stories of what was once a posh midtown home, Foxy is a favorite sit-and-work space for students of the Savannah College of Art and Design. The courtyard hosts shows of all sorts and beckons everyone outside in nice weather. The cafe doubles as a hip print gallery, and the owners recently opened an eclectic shop in the house next door, featuring art, gifts, and coffee-making accoutrements. Foxy's sister store, Coffee Fox on W. Broughton Street, caters to Historic District tourists and Downtown businessfolk. At either location, make sure to try a pull of the signature cold brew.

Foxy Loxy Cafe
1919 Bull St., 912-401-0543
foxyloxycafe.com

Coffee Fox
102 W. Broughton St., 912-401-0399
thecoffeefox.com

HEAD DOWN UNDER
FOR BREAKFAST

Collins Quarter started out as the hot new coffee spot in Savannah, but soon its stellar kitchen made it a go-to meal stop as well. Owned and operated by native Australians, Collins Quarter is based on down-under cafes, where good food, drink, and service come standard. Visit more than once and there's a good chance that a barista will remember your order, if not your name. For coffee, try the Flat White, an espresso topped with microfoam. For food, you can't go wrong with anything from the diverse menu, which features a mix of Southern and Australian standards. And linger a little while to take in Collins Quarter's ambiance. The owners sank a small fortune into renovating the prime corner location, importing fixtures and accents from the world over, paying close attention to every architectural detail and flourish.

151 Bull St., 912-777-4147
thecollinsquarter.com

EAT LIKE THE LOCALS DID...
NINETY YEARS AGO

Tucked into a quiet corner of Savannah's Historic District, the Crystal Beer Parlor may not see as much tourist traffic as establishments in the thick of things, but locals have sought out the Parlor's brews and burgers for generations. Craft beer fans will find an admirable rotation on tap, including several varieties from local breweries. For those looking to truly experience the space's history, then the Beers of Our Fathers menu might be for you, featuring bottles and cans of the same cheap stuff your dad used to drink. No trip to the Parlor is complete without the Classic Crystal Burger and a side of hand-cut fries. The current owners have expanded the menu, too, so you can choose from beers and meals for every mood.

301 W. Jones St., 912-349-1000
crystalbeerparlor.com

CONQUER THE
CONQUISTADOR

If there's one thing that most Savannahians can agree on, it's Zunzi's. The local-favorite restaurant serves varied fare out of what might be the smallest storefront in Savannah, but you can't miss it. The line of customers stretches halfway down the block at lunchtime. The most famous menu item is the Conquistador, a sandwich made with Zunzi's absolutely perfect roast chicken, lettuce, and tomato on French bread. Then they slather the whole thing with Zunzi's extra-special sauce. This isn't just the best sandwich in Savannah—it ranks among the best in America. But you don't have to take my word for it. It earned a spot in the top three in a national sandwich competition. If you're in the mood for an entree, Zunzi's delivers on that front, too, with killer lasagna, cottage pie, and the roast chicken over rice or mashed potatoes. And don't forget the South African iced tea.

108 E. York St., 912-443-9555
zunzis.com

TAKE YOUR TACOS
UP A NOTCH AT TEQUILA'S TOWN

All cantinas are not created equal. Tequila's Town Mexican Restaurant has only been around a few years, but it's already vaulted the competition to claim the top spot as Savannah's favorite Tex-Mex fare. In addition to the expected menu items, T-Town, as downtowners call it, offers a whole category of regional entrees plus unique originals. Savor the Mole Poblano, on-bone chicken smothered in Tequila's signature mole sauce, a subtle blend of chilies and chocolate. Original creations range from the shredded pork Piggy Burrito to the change-of-pace tortilla-wrapped Cheese Steak. Of course, you'll also find the old standards, tacos and burritos and fajitas. Most importantly, don't be afraid to double-dip those nachos. Each guest receives a ramekin of T-Town's absolutely perfect salsa, and refills are always on the house.

109 Whitaker St., 912-236-3222

7360 Skidaway Rd., Sandfly, 912-226-3307

tequilastown.com

GET IN LINE
FOR SOUTHERN COOKING

If you drive down the west end of Jones Street on any weekday around 11 a.m., chances are you'll notice a queue, sometimes a hundred people deep, winding up to the door of a nondescript townhome. That door leads to the Dining Room of Mrs. Wilkes' Boarding House, the most popular Savannah spot for authentic Southern eats. The titular Mrs. Wilkes started the business in 1943, and her reputation for serving the most delicious homecooked meals grew into something of a phenomenon. Today, the Dining Room continues Mrs. Wilkes's legacy. Once you make it through the line, you'll sit at one of a dozen communal tables filled with platters full of food. Savor Southern staples including black-eyed peas, collard greens, okra and tomatoes, and what might be the best fried chicken in the universe. If there was ever a meal worth waiting in line for, you can find it on the tables at Mrs. Wilkes'.

107 W. Jones St., 912-232-5997
mrswilkes.com

CLAIM YOUR SLICE
OF THE PIE

Any fan of Americanized Italian knows that the best pizza can be found in restaurants worthy of the term "joint." Fortunately, Downtown Savannah is home to two such establishments. Up first, check out Vinnie van Gogo's in the corner of City Market. Vinnie's bakes massive slices of Neapolitan-style pizza, as well as whole pies, for hungry downtowners and tourists. They're open until at least 11:30 p.m. to serve the bar-hopping crowd, too. Cash only, though, so hit the ATM before you order. On the other side of Downtown, Screamin' Mimi's tosses Jersey-style pizza, plus some of Savannah's best subs and huge orders of pasta. Instead of bare walls, chalkboards keep kids of all ages entertained while the meals are made to order. Both joints deliver, but no pizza tastes better than a slice served in the right setting.

Vinnie van Gogo's
317 W. Bryan St., 912-233-6394
vinnievangogo.com

Screamin' Mimi's
513 E. Oglethorpe Ave., 912-236-2744
screaminmimispizza.com

DIVE IN FOR AN
ALL-AMERICAN MEAL

Several establishments call the old Chatham Artillery building at the south end of Forsyth Park home, including the Sentient Bean and Brighter Day Natural Foods. American Legion Post 135 has been there longest of all. While a Legion might not be the first place you would think to recommend to a Savannah visitor, the bar is open to the public, and in-house diner Betty Bomber's has been dishing out all-American fare since 2012. The restaurant staff sports 1940s-style outfits and pinned-up hairdos, but don't think it's just a gimmick. You can order any of a dozen delicious old-school favorites from the menu. Keep it simple with a classic burger or Salisbury steak sandwich. Turn to tacos or the fried cod BLT for a modern twist. And sample a true piece of military nostalgia with the colorfully named "Sh*t on a Shingle." Whatever you order, make sure you add gravy to the fries.

1108 Bull St., 912-272-9326
bettybombers.com

DINE LIKE A PIRATE

No family trip to Savannah can be called complete without a visit to the Pirates' House. Situated in Trustees Garden, a plot of land originally set aside for experimental farming by Georgia's founder, James Edward Oglethorpe, the Pirates' House is one of the city's few intact Colonial structures. It started out as an inn for sailors, and yes, it most likely boarded at least a few pirates. An underground tunnel (unfortunately closed to the public) leads directly from the restaurant to the Savannah River, and there are tales of drunken sailors being shanghaied to ships, only to come to their senses far out at sea. You won't come face to face with any kidnappers during your meal, but don't be surprised if a costumed pirate pays a visit to the table. Blending a kid-friendly pirate theme, quality Southern eats, and a building that dates to the early Colonial era, the Pirates' House has something to offer for every seat in the minivan.

20 E. Broad St., 912-233-5757
thepirateshouse.com

YOUR ISLAND OASIS
AT LUNCHTIME

To be fair, Tybee's North Beach Bar & Grill is little more than a shack nestled between the walls of old Fort Screven and a beachside parking lot. But on an island as quirky as Tybee, a shack is where you'll find some of the best grub in the region. The chefs behind the menu can claim a gourmet pedigree, offering seafood favorites and a whole selection of high-end sandwiches at lunchtime. The crab cakes have earned a legendary status among Tybee's residents, and the cheeseburger should tempt anyone away from the fresh seafood offerings. Just a walk over the dunes from a now-popular stretch of beach, the restaurant has both an indoor and an outdoor bar, refueling sunbathers and providing a brief respite from the heat.

33 Meddin Dr., Tybee Island, 912-786-4442
northbeachbarandgrill.net

SATISFY YOUR
SWEET TOOTH

If you're eating out in Downtown Savannah, save room for one of the artisanal creations at Lulu's Chocolate Bar. Since it opened more than a decade ago, Lulu's has become the city's go-to spot for deluxe desserts and digestifs. A glass-fronted cooler full of delectable edibles greets you as you enter the front door, from cakes and cheesecakes to tortes and tarts. And you won't find a better crème brûlée anywhere. The bar staff has also concocted a whole range of dessert martinis, including the signature Lulutini, a luscious mix of chocolate vodka, chocolate liqueur, Crème de Cacao, and Lulu's own sipping chocolate. If that's too much of a sugar rush, the bar comes fully stocked and ready to mix your preferred after-dinner cocktail.

42 MLK Jr. Blvd., 912-480-4564
luluschocolatebar.com

SAVE ROOM
FOR CUPCAKES

The warm scent of fresh pastries beckons you through the front door of Back in the Day Bakery. Situated south of the Historic District in Starland, the bakery caters to midtowners looking for coffee and a bite in the morning and serves as a favorite meeting spot for locals throughout the day. Try a scone or muffin, or build your own breakfast biscuit from a seasonal selection of ingredients. Whatever you order, save room for one of the bakery's famous cupcakes (and make sure you get there early, before the daily batch sells out). Back in the Day has grown into more than just a local phenomenon, too. Proprietors Cheryl and Griffith Day's first cookbook went on to be a *New York Times* bestseller, and the sequel continues to spread the good news of Southern-style baking to a national audience.

2403 Bull St., 912-495-9292
backinthedaybakery.com

NEXT STOP:
FINE SOUTHERN DINING

The Grey exploded onto Savannah's dining scene in 2014 and has earned dozens of glowing writeups in national publications ranging from the *New York Times* to *Cosmopolitan*. Locally, the Grey earned a reputation as the place to be seen, serving gourmet meals in a uniquely upscale atmosphere. Set in what was once an Art Deco Greyhound bus station dating from 1938, the main dining room might be the chicest spot in town, and the Diner Bar up front serves small bites and a selection of classy cocktails in a more casual atmosphere. Executive Chef Mashama Bailey hails from Waynesboro, Georgia, and combines her downhome Southern cooking heritage with a New York City culinary education. You've never tasted soul food like this.

109 MLK Jr. Blvd., 912-662-5999
thegreyrestaurant.com

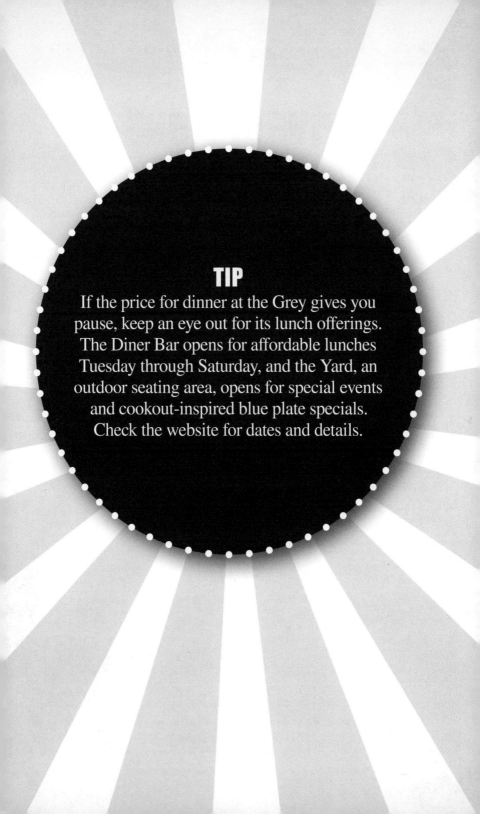

TIP

If the price for dinner at the Grey gives you pause, keep an eye out for its lunch offerings. The Diner Bar opens for affordable lunches Tuesday through Saturday, and the Yard, an outdoor seating area, opens for special events and cookout-inspired blue plate specials. Check the website for dates and details.

FIVE OPTIONS
FOR FUSION

When it comes to Asian-inspired fusion in Savannah, one restaurant group has the genre covered. Ele and the Chef run a double handful of favorite eateries, and the group has singlehandedly elevated the level of cool cuisine in the city. Try the Tuk Tuk Noodles or Lemongrass Chicken at Fire Street Food. Flying Monk has your favorite noodle dishes covered. Head across Broughton Street to Chive for a whole selection of seafood, including a raw bar. The Vault, set in a renovated bank building near Starland, serves up a spicy variety of hot dishes plus a complete sushi menu. If you're out on the islands, make a reservation at Ele Fine Fusion for a luxurious dining experience. With a restaurant for every taste and budget, what unifies Ele and the Chef's endeavors is quality. You're sure to find a new favorite meal at whichever restaurant you choose.

Fire Street Food
13 E. Perry Ln., 912-234-7776
firestreetfood.com

Flying Monk Noodle Bar
5 W. Broughton St., 912-232-8888
flywiththemonk.com

Chive Sea Bar & Lounge
4 W. Broughton St., 912-233-1748
chivelounge.com

The Vault Kitchen and Market
2112 Bull St., 912-201-1950
vaultkitchen.com

Ele Fine Fusion
7815 US Highway 80 E., 912-898-2221
elesavannah.com

KEEP IT SIMPLE
WITH A SAVANNAH STAPLE

B&D Burgers operates two downtown locations only a couple blocks away from each other. That alone should give you an idea of the popularity of this Savannah mainstay. B&D's formula is simple: serve up tasty burgers and several varieties of fries, including a fry of the day, all in a no-frills environment. Opt for a classic with the Telfair, a local version of the bacon cheeseburger. The Wormsloe comes to your table via the Deep South, topped with pimento cheese and a fried green tomato. You can build your own burger, too, using any combination of dozens of toppings, including the fan-favorite fried egg. In addition to the standard Angus beef, order any burger made with bison, elk, turkey, or a three-bean veggie patty. The Congress Street location features a large beer garden for outdoor dining and a huge projection TV, perfect for watching the late game.

13 E. Broughton St., 912-231-0986

209 W. Congress St., 912-238-8315

bdburgers.net

EAT, DRINK, AND
BE SOCIAL

Sure, you could go anywhere for burgers and beer, but there's one place that makes this quintessential American dining experience decidedly Savannahian. Green Truck Neighborhood Pub makes grub with a Savannah-centric focus. The beef is sourced from nearby Brooklet, Georgia, and they buy in-season produce from area farms. Heck, even the menus are made by local printers. But the pub's dedication to authenticity doesn't stop here. Every item is made by hand, from the french fries to the ketchup you dip them in. Craft brews pour from every tap. And a selection of six fresh-made salads will keep the herbivore in your party well fed, too. Most important, though, is the community atmosphere. The proprietors love bringing people together for a great meal, and no Savannah experience is complete without a bit of socializing thrown in.

2430 Habersham St., 912-234-5885
greentruckpub.com

DINE IN SAVANNAH'S
ONLY COLONIAL MANSION

The Olde Pink House, named for the distinctive color of its stucco exterior, has occupied the corner across from Reynolds Square since 1771, making it the only surviving Colonial mansion in the city. The mansion was built for James Habersham, Jr., a member of the same Habersham family who helped found Savannah. Today, though, the Pink House is known as much for food as it is for history. Fine diners flock to intimate settings in the mansion's resplendent rooms, and you're likely to find the local elite alongside tourists alongside teen couples decked out for prom. The chefs craft delectable versions of Southern favorites, as well as Southern-inspired originals. Don't miss the downstairs tavern, a cozy bar that may or may not be haunted by the ghost of James Habersham himself.

23 Abercorn St., 912-232-4286
plantersinnsavannah.com/the-olde-pink-house

HOWEVER YOU
PRONOUNCE IT, ORDER A GYRO
ON RIVER STREET

Jie-ro or yee-ro. Whichever way you say it, there's no better place to order one—or any Greek dish—than Olympia Cafe. Just behind City Hall on River Street, Olympia is split into two restaurants in one. Walk through the left door and order at the counter, or reserve a table on the other side of the restaurant for a sit-down meal. While the sit-down side provides a more upscale setting, they welcome the casual River Street crowd. Olympia's specialties include flaky spanakotiropita, hearty pastitsio, and dolmades. Order the Greek Duo and get any two entrees plus sides, including lemony oven-roasted potatoes. There's also a whole menu section for sandwiches, where you can choose from gyros and kebabs. For fans of calamari, you'd be hard pressed to find a tastier appetizer anywhere.

5 E. River St., 912-233-3131
olympiacafe.net

HEAD FARTHER SOUTH
FOR SOUTHERN COOKIN'

While there are options for Southern fare in the Historic District, locals know that two of the best Southern eateries reside outside Downtown proper. Sisters of the New South cooks up pure, simple soul food. You can't go wrong with the legendary fried chicken or turkey wings, and they serve the best oxtails in the area. Whatever you order from Sisters' cafeteria-style counter, know that the plate will be heaped high with goodness. Sweet Potatoes Restaurant whips up its own variety of Southern favorites, as well as original dishes with a Southern accent. The pork chop is grilled to perfection, or try something new with the pecan-encrusted tilapia, topped with peach cranberry salsa. Southerners know that sides make the meal, so at either restaurant, pair your entree with downhome classics such as collard greens or black-eyed peas.

Sisters of the New South
2605 Skidaway Rd., 912-335-2761
thesistersofthenewsouth.com

Sweet Potatoes Restaurant
6825 Waters Ave., 912-352-3434
facebook.com/sweetpotatoeskitchen

A SCOOP 100
YEARS IN THE MAKING

What's that queue on Broughton Street? Those are just the people lined up outside Leopold's Ice Cream. Leopold's has been creating Savannah's favorite frozen treats for nearly a century, serving up fond memories to generations of locals. Even today, the shop still showcases the quaint charm of your grandparents' era. Friendly staff in red aprons and paper hats scoop out original flavors, from classic vanilla to new favorites like Rum Bisque. Whichever flavor you choose, know that Leopold's handcrafts the ice cream in Downtown Savannah based on old family recipes, some of them even older than the shop itself. Stratton Leopold, the most recent member of the family to serve as proprietor, also made a name for himself as a Hollywood producer. Props and posters from his many movies decorate the shop, so once you make it through the line, take a minute to look around.

212 E. Broughton St., 912-234-4442
leopoldsicecream.com

TASTE ALL OF
SAVANNAH'S BEST AT ONE EVENT

Savannahians love to eat and drink, so it should come as no surprise that we created a festival just to celebrate these two favorite pastimes. The Savannah Food and Wine Festival originated with a three-hour dining event featuring local chefs and restaurants. That small gathering has grown into a week-long celebration of all things culinary, culminating with Taste of Savannah, a massive open-air festival serving fine food and drink to thousands of guests. Leading up to the big day, you can attend food and beverage tastings, cocktail competitions, and even lectures for those who want to learn a few tricks of the foodie trade from the masters. The Food and Wine Fest comes around every November, and tickets can sell out fast, so reserve your spot at the table early.

savannahfoodandwinefest.com

DRINK LIKE A
COMMANDER IN CHIEF

If part of your Savannah plan is to take in our legendary bar culture, then make Abe's on Lincoln your first stop. The space has seen several iterations over the years, but it's always been a bar, making it the oldest watering hole in town. Decades ago, the space went by the name Jim Collins and drew a crowd of counterculture locals alongside at least a couple of unconfirmed sightings of Bob Dylan. Today, Abe's welcomes folks from the neighborhood as well as out-of-towners on walking pub crawls. The dark, low-ceilinged space harkens back to a different era of drinking, but that just makes it cozy in a way that modern bars aren't. Plus, its distance from the hubbub of City Market gives it a more relaxed, social atmosphere. If you're feeling artistically inclined, sketch a presidential portrait of the titular Abe on a cocktail napkin, and the staff will add it to the hundreds hanging from the walls and ceiling.

17 Lincoln St., 912-349-0525
abesonlincoln.com

TOAST TO AN AUTHENTIC
SAVANNAH EXPERIENCE

Jimmy Carter once climbed atop the bar at Pinkie Masters to toast the bar's founder, but this rich history couldn't save the establishment from closing its doors in 2016. Fortunately, new owners swooped in to claim the space, spruced everything up a bit, and reopened the establishment as The Original Pinkie Master's in its former state of dive bar glory. Expect cheap beer and liquor/soda combos in plastic cups, but the new proprietors also added wine and batch cocktails to the menu. Locals still crowd the bar more than tourists, and happy hour hosts a mix of tie-loosened businessfolk and oddball eccentrics. More than anything else, Pinkie's offers an experience, and it's probably the best place left in Savannah to see the city as it was when John Berendt penned *Midnight in the Garden of Good and Evil*. Make sure you read the brass plaque set in the bar, marking the spot where an American president once stood.

318 Drayton St., 912-999-7106
theoriginalsavannah.com

GET SCHOOLED
IN SCOTCH

If you're looking for a dram of the good stuff, look no further than Molly MacPherson's. This Scottish pub boasts the city's best selection of Scotch, one of the most extensive in the whole region. A dedicated whisky menu features dozens and dozens of single malt Scotches, covering every region and style, plus a selection of premium Scotch flights for your sampling pleasure. If you're a Scotch newbie, or if you're just seeking a fresh flavor, the barkeeps know a thing or two about their beverages, and they'll be happy to guide you in the right direction. Don't be worried if Scotch isn't your thing. Molly's is far from stuffy and will serve up just about anything you can think to order. The food menu has a wide selection of A+ pub food, too, from the delectable Scottish meatloaf to the Aberdeen Black Watch Burger, which is a dark horse candidate for the best burger in Savannah.

311 W. Congress St., 912-239-9600
macphersonspub.com

BOOZE WITH A VIEW

People visit Savannah for a variety of reasons, but two of the most popular are to take in the city's beauty and to hop the city's bars. Fortunately, there are a couple of rooftop establishments that allow you to do both at same time. Rocks on the Roof at the Bohemian Hotel and Top Deck at the Cotton Sail Hotel stand side by side between Bay Street and River Street. Both overlook the Historic District on one side and the Savannah River on the other. And both welcome locals and tourists with open arms. Head to the west side of either building to watch the sun set behind the bridge, or line up along the north wall to wait for one of the container ships that navigate the channel day and night—Savannah is the fourth busiest port in the United States, after all. Both bars are stocked with whatever you need to tide you over while you wait.

Rocks on the Roof at the Bohemian Hotel
102 W. Bay St., 912-721-3800
bohemianhotelsavannah.com

Top Deck at the Cotton Sail Hotel
125 W. River St., 912-436-6828
topdeckbar.com

DOWN A PINT OF
LOCAL SUDS

Savannah came late to the craft beer craze, but two outstanding breweries have bubbled up on the west side of Downtown over the past few years. Southbound Brewing Co. drew its first brew in 2013 and has since exploded onto the scene with a variety of beers available at most local bars and package shops. For the pale ale crowd, try Southbound's Hop'lin IPA, and for something less hoppy, a six pack of Scattered Sun Wit always makes a splash at parties. Service Brewing Company, veteran owned and operated, opened just a year after Southbound, and its beers also quickly found a home behind Savannah's bars. Service brews a couple of styles of pale ale year-round, as well as a Bohemian-style pilsner that's a great change of pace. Keep an eye out for seasonal and special offerings from both breweries, and check their websites for brewery tours, tastings, and special events.

Service Brewing Co.
574 Indian St., 912-358-1002
servicebrewing.com

Southbound Brewing Co.
107 E. Lathrop Ave., 912-335-1737
southboundbrewingco.com

DRINK UP, YOU'RE IRISH

Everyone in Savannah may be Irish for St. Patrick's Day, but for those who can claim green blood year-round, there's always a pint of Guinness near at hand. Kevin Barry's Irish Pub on River Street opened in 1980, and it remains the preferred pub of old-school locals. Enjoy a drink or a meal—Kevin Barry's offers a selection of pub food well beyond just the usual shepherd's pie—or step into the listening room for live Irish music seven nights a week. Upstairs, the Hall of Heroes honors the people who've served in the U.S. military and is a favorite stop for active-duty personnel and veterans. If small and cozy is more your style, then try O'Connell's Irish Pub. Tucked into a nondescript corner just off Broughton Street, it serves the best curated selection of Irish whiskies in town.

Kevin Barry's Irish Pub
117 W. River St., 912-233-9626
kevinbarrys.com

O'Connell's Irish Pub
42 Drayton St., 912-231-2298

BUST A MOVE
AT SAVANNAH'S #1 GAY BAR

Drag shows, dancing, drinks, and more! Club One rises three stories over Bay Street and is as much a Savannah monument as it is a gay bar. Opened in 1988, the club has anchored the city's nightlife ever since, playing host to locals and tourists alike. The dance floor has been consistently voted as the best in the city for more than two decades, and it welcomes anyone with an itch to move to the beat. Both the bar and the Bay Street Theatre upstairs host shows and concerts of all sorts. The late Lady Chablis (made famous in John Berendt's *Midnight in the Garden of Good and Evil* and for playing herself in the film) called Club One home base, and a roster of A-list drag queens carry on her legacy several nights a week.

1 Jefferson St., 912-232-0200
clubone-online.com

BUY BOOZE WHERE YOUR
GRANDPARENTS DID

Planning a party or stocking the bar in a vacation rental? Johnnie Ganem's Package and Wine Shop has been furnishing Savannah's homes with the finest spirits since 1942, making it a true piece of local history. In addition to the liquor store, the space once housed a bar, lounge, and soda fountain. Three generations of Ganems later, and the shop is still going strong in the heart of Downtown. The focus now is solely on booze, with one of the best selections of beer, wine, and the hard stuff around. Find local beers from Southbound, Service, and Coastal Empire Beer Company. Bring home a bottle of regional spirits such as Savannah Bourbon (distilled in Milledgeville, Georgia) or Daufuskie Island Rum. And if you need help choosing a bottle of wine, the knowledgeable staff can help you uncork a crowd-pleaser at your next party.

501 Habersham St., 912-233-3032
johnnieganem.com

FIND A NEW
FAVORITE COCKTAIL

You might have to spend a little time exploring before you locate Savannah's best bar for cocktails. The entrance to Alley Cat Lounge, one of the newest drink spots Downtown, is tucked into the backside of the 200 block of Broughton Street. Enter through the semi-secret door in the lane, and take the steps down to discover a quiet, intimate space. And get ready to spend at least a few minutes with the menu. Printed as a newspaper, it features more than 100 cocktails, each a tried and true variation on the classics. No drinkable dessert concoctions here. These are cocktails for people who love their liquor. For example, there are four cocktails in the Manhattan category alone, from the original formula to a New Orleans-style Vieux Carre. And no place in Savannah mixes a better Sazerac, America's original cocktail.

207 W. Broughton St. (entrance in lane), 912-677-0548
alleycatsavannah.com

ROLL UP TO A FAVORITE
SAVANNAH PUB

The Rail Pub proudly calls itself a dive bar, and it's played host to Savannah's no-frills drinkers since it opened in the 1990s. The history of the building goes back more than a hundred years before that, and it even supposedly served as a brothel in what was once the city's red light district. Today, the Rail specializes in cheap beer and mixed drinks. A host of regulars claim the bar for weekday happy hours and free peanuts. Play a game of darts in the back room, or step out to the courtyard when the weather's nice. The Rail added an open-air beer garden in what was once a vacant lot next door, expanding its outdoor space several times over. Friday and Saturday nights find the Rail packed with townies and tourists, but if you're willing to fight the crowd, it's still one of the favorite spots for Savannah's bar-hoppers.

405 W. Congress St., 912-238-1311
therailpub.com

A BRITISH PUB WITH
A SOUTHERN ACCENT

The moment you step off Bay Street into Churchill's GastroPub
& Taphouse, you'll notice the towering bar on the left. Ornately
crafted out of dark-stained wood, it feels like something ripped
straight out of the Old Country and dropped in the heart of
Savannah. Dozens of liquor taps line the wall, including a decent
selection of Scotches, plus twenty beers on draught. Winston's
Wine Cellar occupies the basement level and is one of the city's
few dedicated wine bars. In fair weather, head up to the rooftop
terrace. Nestled on the backside of Churchill's and overlooking
Johnson Square, it's a great stop when you're out with a larger
party. Churchill's also serves a full selection of traditional and
contemporary pub fare that would be sure to satisfy even the
British Bulldog himself.

13 W. Bay St., 912-232-8501
thebritishpub.com

CHECK IN FOR QUALITY
COCKTAILS

If the only time you think to hit up a hotel's bar is when you're staying there, think again. 22 Square in Andaz Savannah mixes some of the best cocktails in town. Set just off Andaz's lobby and overlooking Ellis Square, the bar draws a who's who of Savannahians and works just as well to cap a formal evening out as it does for a more casual gathering of friends. Sit at the bar and strike up a conversation, or claim one of the several lounge areas for a larger group. The bar stocks a select list of premium liquors and prides itself on products that you can't find anywhere else in town. The cocktail list changes seasonally, but the East of Hudson, 22 Square's version of a classic Manhattan, always earns top billing.

14 Barnard St., 912-233-2116
savannah.andaz.hyatt.com

CRUISE DOWN
CONGRESS STREET

The Congress Street strip covers just three blocks between MLK Jr. Boulevard and Whitaker Street, but you can find more bars there per square foot than most anywhere else in America. Start just around the corner on MLK Jr. Boulevard at Rogue Water, then tackle Congress Street Social Club, Boomy's, and the Rail without ever having to cross a street. As Congress Street runs behind City Market, hit up Molly MacPherson's, Treehouse, or the bars at fine dining restaurants Garibaldi's and a'lure. You'll probably need a belly-fill at this point, so stop at Wild Wing Cafe or B&D Burgers for a bite and a beer. Overlooking Ellis Square, the Jinx and Barrel House South serve up drinks and live music. Top it all off with a slice of pizza—or three—from late-night mainstay Sweet Melissa's, at the corner of Congress and Whitaker.

Rogue Water
38 MLK Jr. Blvd., 912-349-1549

Congress Street Social Club
411 W. Congress St., 912-238-1985
congressstreetsocialclub.com

Boomy's Bar
409 W. Congress St., 912-436-6660
facebook.com/BoomysBar

The Rail Pub
405 W. Congress St., 912-238-1311
therailpub.com

Molly MacPherson's
311 W. Congress St., 912-239-9600
macphersonspub.com

Treehouse
309 W. Saint Julian St., 912-660-0033
facebook.com/TreehouseSavannah

Garibaldi's
315 W. Congress St., 912-232-7118
garibaldisavannah.com

a'lure
309 W. Congress St., 912-233-2111
aluresavannah.com

Wild Wing Cafe
27 Barnard St., 912-790-9464
wildwingcafe.com

B&D Burgers
209 W. Congress St., 912-238-8315
bdburgers.net

The Jinx
127 W. Congress St., 912-236-2281
facebook.com/thejinx912

Barrelhouse South
125 W. Congress St., 912-662-576
barrelhousesouth.com

Sweet Melissa's
103 W. Congress St., 912-341-0093
facebook.com/sweetmelissasga

UNCORK AN EVENING
OUT WITH FRIENDS

Looking for a glass of fine wine? Then say *bon jour* to Circa 1875, a French bistro and gastropub tucked into twin storefronts on Whitaker Street. Circa maintains an extensive wine list, and the bar and wait staff can help even wine novices find the perfect selection. In the bistro, pair your wine with Circa's French-inspired entrées, including one of the best local options for duck. The restaurant sees its fair share of fancy dates, but the atmosphere is laid back enough for more casual diners, as well. Though relatively small, the pub side of Circa has become a favorite Savannah social spot, with several large tables in addition to the bar itself. Split one of Circa's scrumptious hors d'oeuvres, and share a bottle of wine with friends.

48 Whitaker St., 912-443-1875
circa1875.com

GO RETRO AT EL-ROCKO

Few establishments open to as much excitement as El-Rocko Lounge. After the beloved dive bar/music venue Hang Fire was forced to close, the proprietors moved one block down Whitaker Street and started fresh with El-Rocko. Their new digs glitter with retro charm: mid-century-inspired seating, chic fixtures, and foil wallpaper in geometric patterns. Music still plays a central role, and you can find indie acts from Savannah and beyond, from punk to surf to rock 'n' roll, taking El-Rocko's stage several nights a week. For the drinking crowd, El-Rocko stocks the bar with premium beer and spirits. Sip one of its signature cocktails, including several unique barrel-aged options served on draught. Whether you're there for drinks or a show, know that you've chosen the city's hippest spot.

117 Whitaker St., 912-495-5808
facebook.com/pachinko21

Photo credit: Geoff Johnson

MUSIC AND ENTERTAINMENT

CATCH AN OLD FAVORITE
FLICK ON THE BIG SCREEN

The glamorous Lucas Theatre languished in the latter part of the 20th century, but thanks to a group of dedicated preservationists, it rang in the new millennium with all the style it showcased at its 1921 premiere. Now home to year-round concerts and performances, the Lucas may be best loved by locals for its annual film series. Featured films range from cult classics such as *Big Trouble in Little China* to blockbusting favorites like *Jurassic Park* to timeless gems from cinema's golden age. If you find yourself sweltering on a summer day, the early-evening showtimes—usually 7:00 p.m.—provide a perfect respite from the heat. The Lucas was the first public building with air conditioning in Savannah, after all. Plus, the concession stand serves beer in addition to the usual theater fare, so you can catch a movie and start your evening out all at the same time.

32 Abercorn St., 912-525-5040
lucastheatre.com

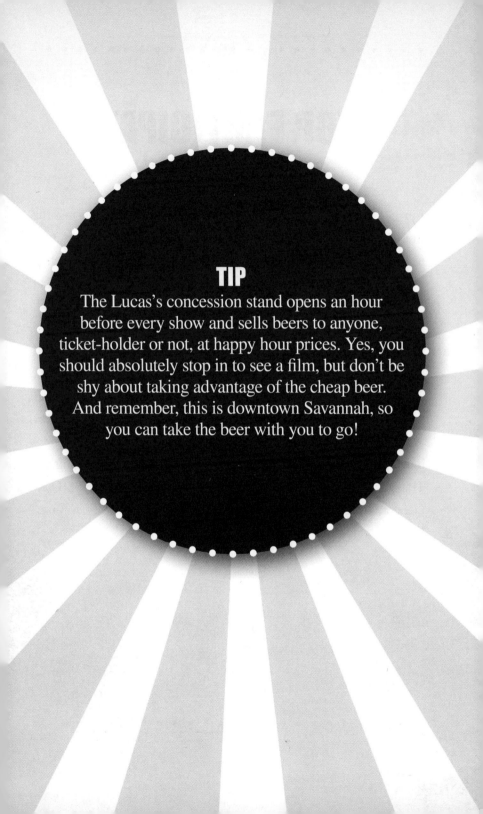

TIP

The Lucas's concession stand opens an hour before every show and sells beers to anyone, ticket-holder or not, at happy hour prices. Yes, you should absolutely stop in to see a film, but don't be shy about taking advantage of the cheap beer. And remember, this is downtown Savannah, so you can take the beer with you to go!

STOP, PARTICIPATE,
AND LISTEN

For a long time, Savannah was bypassed by bands touring the Southeast. Despite our proximity to Athens's legendary music scene, as well as major cities such as Atlanta and Jacksonville, Savannah just didn't have the draw for up-and-coming acts. The city's musical reputation blossomed, though, thanks in large part to the Savannah Stopover Music Festival. Stopover takes advantage of Savannah's location along Interstate 95 to lure East Coast bands for pit stops and performances on their way to the massive SXSW festival in Austin, Texas. This simple idea has grown into a full-fledged festival, and for one long weekend in early March each year, Savannah becomes America's hot spot for showcasing indie music. Past performers have gone on to fame and acclaim, including Grimes, of Montreal, The War On Drugs, Future Islands, Mac Demarco, Wye Oak, Generationals, Ra Ra Riot, Oberhofer, Reptar, and countless more. Keep an eye out for the line-up announced each fall.

savannahstopover.com

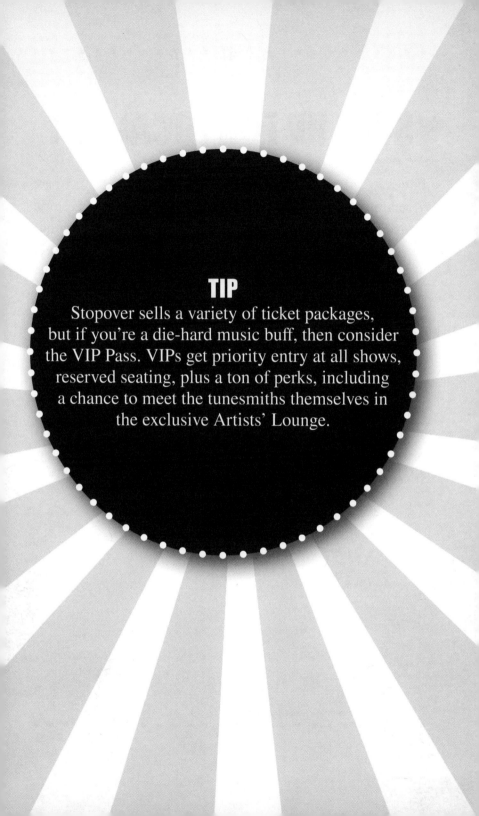

TIP

Stopover sells a variety of ticket packages, but if you're a die-hard music buff, then consider the VIP Pass. VIPs get priority entry at all shows, reserved seating, plus a ton of perks, including a chance to meet the tunesmiths themselves in the exclusive Artists' Lounge.

STEP UP FOR LOCAL ART

For every art gallery you stumble upon in Savannah, there are several tucked into odd corners or situated outside the Historic District. To get a taste of everything Savannah's art scene has to offer, hit up First Fridays in Starland, a monthly gallery-hop centered in Savannah's bohemian Starland District. You'll discover a stellar range of local artists exhibiting their work in numerous galleries, plus arty shops and not a few restaurants. Solo and group shows cover the whole range of artistic mediums: painting, printmaking, photography, sculpture, and even video and digital installations. In addition to the art, attendees can enjoy live music, food and drink, and all sorts of activities on stops along the way. Like most events in Savannah, First Fridays bring out the city's social side. You'll find it's easy to make new friends, especially if you're inclined to artistic conversations.

artrisesavannah.org

TUNE UP FOR
WORLD-CLASS MUSIC

Savannah's most comprehensive musical experience can be found at the Savannah Music Festival. Founded in 1989, it has burgeoned into a world-class event, expanding both the number and quality of concerts presented in March and April of each year. The festival has lured the likes of jazz greats Wayne Shorter and Joshua Redman; classical ensembles all the way up to the Atlanta Symphony Orchestra; masters of Americana, world music, and bluegrass; and outright rock and pop acts, including Asleep at the Wheel and the Avett Brothers. Several concerts are held daily throughout the run of the festival, and most of Savannah's best venues take part. Devoted locals and music fans from all over snatch up tickets as soon as they go on sale, so order early before the shows you want to see sell out.

savannahmusicfestival.org

PLUG IN FOR PULSE

Is it technology or is it art? In the case of PULSE Art + Technology Festival, the answer is both! This annual January festival, headquartered at Telfair Museums' Jepson Center, celebrates the intersection of aesthetics and electronics, with an emphasis on interactive exhibitions. Past features have included Daniel Rozin's transforming mirrors, which cast a shadowy "reflection" of the viewer by manipulating hundreds of everyday objects with small motors; multimedia performances, including an audiovisual reimagining of *Beowulf*; and live concerts by digital-savvy musicians. Plus there's always a selection of arty video games, lectures, workshops, and more. Check out the exhibitions during the day for free, and visit the Telfair website for passes to the evening PULSE festivities and special events.

207 E. York St., 912-790-8800
telfair.org/pulse

YOU'RE IN LUCK
FOR LOCAL ROCK 'N' ROLL

Known for late starts and loud speakers, the Jinx has anchored Savannah's rock scene since 2003. Even before that, the space housed another legendary music venue, the Velvet Elvis, and the walls reverberate with the echoes of thousands of concerts. On show nights, you can spot The Jinx by the cluster of black-clad smokers out front, and you'll probably hear it even before that. Inside, the narrow space funnels everyone to the front of the stage, though you're welcome to sit at the bar or get there early to claim one of the booths, stage right. Though you'll need to pay a cover and get a hand stamp for shows, the bar is open most evenings for happy hour specials, and contrary to the rollicking atmosphere later in the night, it makes a great spot to chill with friends.

127 W. Congress St., 912-236-2281
facebook.com/thejinx912

REDISCOVER
A CLASSIC MELODY

When the old Savannah Symphony Orchestra folded in 2003, it seemed like the end of live classical music in the city. Fortunately, no one told that to Peter Shannon, an Irish conductor who came to Savannah by way of Germany. Shannon moved quickly to form the Savannah Philharmonic, reestablishing the city's symphonic culture and then some. A professional orchestra and chorus, staffed by expert musicians from around the region, the Philharmonic performs an extensive season of concerts ranging from classical standards to seasonal pops favorites. The rest of the calendar is filled by chamber performances featuring the Philharmonic's principle players. Tickets start at under $20, and the atmosphere at performances is anything but stuffy. For die-hard music buffs, subscription packages let you enjoy the whole season while earning a few special perks.

savannahphilharmonic.org

TIP

Once a year, the Savannah Philharmonic holds a free outdoor performance at Picnic in the Park. Held in the Forsyth Park band shell, the concert starts with other acts in the afternoon, culminating with the Philharmonic performance in the evening. And don't forget your picnic basket. Savannahians go all out with their spreads, from tents to tables to fine china. You might even spot a chandelier!

STEP INTO ONE OF
AMERICA'S OLDEST SPOTLIGHTS

At first glance, the Art Deco-styled Savannah Theatre appears to be a product of the early twentieth century, but the building can trace its origins back to a debut performance in 1818. That makes it one of the oldest continually operating theaters in the United States. A hurricane and two fires damaged previous iterations of the structure, including the original theater designed by prolific Savannah architect William Jay. Despite these disasters, the site on the northeast corner of Chippewa Square has always been open to the public for live shows and films. Legendary performers such as W. C. Fields and Oscar Wilde showcased their talents to Savannah audiences from the theater's stage, and today a troupe of local actors puts on crowd-pleasing, all-ages musical reviews and seasonal specials.

222 Bull St., 912-233-7764
savannahtheatre.com

TAKE THE MIC
AT MCDONOUGH'S

If your favorite song is the one you sing yourself, then McDonough's Restaurant & Lounge should be your first stop for entertainment. The neighborhood bar features karaoke every night, and Savannah's most talented (or at least enthusiastic) amateur singers take the stage to show their stuff. The song list includes a comprehensive collection of hits and favorites, and you can even find forgotten deep cuts and one-hit wonders. Warm up with weekday happy hours, or cap off a night of carousing Downtown by making McDonough's your last call. The atmosphere is always rowdy and the drinks run cheap, so bring your best singing voice and leave your inhibitions behind.

21 E. McDonough St., 912-233-6136
mcdonoughssavannah.com

EXPERIENCE POETRY
IN PERSON

You might think that poetry isn't your thing, but Spitfire Poetry Group begs to differ. Founded in 2000, Spitfire kicked off the new millennium by bringing together Savannah's creative community, hosting open mics for local poets, rappers, and spoken word artists, as well as bringing in regional and national performers. The performances fall somewhere between literature and theater, with passionate readings and recitations. Yes, appreciative finger-snaps are welcome, but you'll be hard pressed to keep your seat. Hooting, hollering, clapping, and foot stomping are the preferred responses.

facebook.com/spitfireartist

TIP

The group holds regular shows every month, and it cohosts the annual Savannah Spoken Word Festival each spring with several other local literary organizations.

GET PULLED IN
FOR LIVE MUSIC

Looking for a live show without having to fight for Downtown parking? Midtown music lovers claim The Wormhole as their venue of choice. The Wormhole has grown from a neighborhood pub into a major indie music venue since it opened in 2009. In addition to music, the venue serves as a main stop for local and touring comedians and offers open mics, karaoke, and trivia on a weekly basis. The Wormhole prides itself on a friendly, inclusive atmosphere, so come in before a show or stay after for drinks and bar food. The kitchen stays open until 2:45 a.m., making it one of the only places south of the Historic District to silence a grumbling stomach after a late show.

2307 Bull St., 912-713-2855
wormholebar.com

SWING ONTO THE DANCE FLOOR

Jazz fans rejoice! Local swing-lovers can get their fill of traditional jazz from the Fabulous Equinox Orchestra, a seventeen piece big band based out of Savannah. The band's frontmen, Jeremy Davis and Clay Johnson, have played thousands of shows around the world, and listeners can't help but be charmed by their easygoing chemistry. The orchestra brings the swagger of the Rat Pack to energetic and entertaining stage shows and backs up the bluster with top-notch musicianship. You'll recognize most of the classic tunes the band performs, some of which have been jazz standards for nearly a century, but Equinox has mastered original arrangements, giving every note a specific Savannah flavor. The only downside: Equinox has grown so popular it now takes to the road for national tours. Check its calendar for local concerts.

equinoxorchestra.com

Photo credit: The Savannah Bananas

SPORTS AND RECREATION

SAVANNAH
GOES BANANAS FOR BASEBALL

Things looked bleak for baseball in Savannah when our long-time minor league franchise picked up and moved elsewhere. But when a new team came to town, prospects brightened considerably. To bright yellow, in fact. The Savannah Bananas became an instant fan phenomenon when they claimed historic Grayson Stadium as their home field. While the silly name bothered some locals, an inaugural season full of sell-outs showed that what people wanted most from a local team was a home run of fun. The Bananas play in the Coastal Plain League, a summer circuit for current college athletes, and they won the league championship in their first season. Throw in amazing food and drink deals, goofy theatrics, and at least a few players dancing between innings, and you've found the most fun you can have outside on a Savannah summer day.

1401 E. Victory Dr., 912-712-2482
thesavannahbananas.com

DIP YOUR TOES
IN THE ATLANTIC

Tybee Island, the easternmost point in Georgia, lies at the terminus of U.S. Highway 80. Once accessible only by rail, Tybee retains much of its cloistered and quirky charm even today and remains the preferred destination for beach bums from throughout the region. Even in the cooler months, Tybee thrives thanks to a healthy population of year-round residents. Plan your trip to coincide with the annual Pirate Fest or Beach Bum Parade, though be aware that you'll likely be soaked at the latter—water guns are the bums' accessory of choice. Tybee even hosts its own St. Patrick's Day Parade, usually within a few days of the main Savannah celebration. While you won't have any trouble finding a hotel or vacation rental on the island, it's the locals who keep the place authentic, floating a truly excellent drinking and dining scene through the quieter months.

visittybee.com

WHIP YOURSELF
INTO A FRENZY AT THE ROLLER DERBY

If you're looking for the best homegrown athletes in the area, look no further than the Savannah Derby Devils. Savannah's all-stars strap on roller-skates each spring and summer for a series of bouts at the Savannah Civic Center. Since the Devils formed in 2006, the team has grown into one of the most competitive in the region, and they now roll out two full squads each season, plus a development team for aspiring skaters aged eleven to seventeen. Bouts mix family-friendly fandom with a punk rock aesthetic, plus a healthy dose of bone-crunching action. No need to fret if you don't know the first thing about roller derby. The Devils print the rules in the program, and you'll only have to watch a few laps around the track to learn the intricacies of the game.

savannahderby.com

CROSS THE
SAVANNAH RIVER ON FOOT

On any given spring Saturday, you're likely to find a charity footrace weaving through the streets of Downtown Savannah. But the city's marquee race doesn't come until December, when the Savannah Bridge Run crosses the Savannah River and back again, and even back once more for the boldest runners. The bridge reaches 185 feet at its highest point, making for a grueling climb and a wobbly-legged descent. Runners choose one of two races, a 5K or a 10K, and can opt for the Double-Pump, both races back-to-back. While the competition draws serious runners from all over the region, it welcomes athletes of all levels and even encourages costumes with cash prizes for the best dressed. Like all good Savannah events, the Bridge Run ends with a party, featuring brews and Brunswick stew, plus medals for everyone hearty enough to cross the finish line.

savannahbridgerun.com

PACE YOURSELF
FOR THE BIG RACE

The Rock 'n' Roll Marathon series added Savannah as a stop in 2011, and the event now draws more than 10,000 runners and several times that many supporters to the city for one weekend each November. Traditionally a slower time for tourism in the city, the pace picks up considerably that weekend, with many restaurants serving carb-heavy specials the Friday before the race. Saturday sees streets Downtown and beyond blocked off, and before long what seems like an endless stream of runners zigzags through the city. The rock 'n' roll portion of the event showcases both local and touring acts on stages all along the race route. Choose the full- or half-marathon course, or just come Downtown after the race to raise a glass to everyone who managed to earn a medal. Make sure to ask about food and drink discounts for race participants at local restaurants and bars.

runrocknroll.com/savannah

HEAT UP THE RINK

The South isn't known as a hotbed for ice hockey. But for one weekend every January, the Savannah Civic Center becomes headquarters for hockey enthusiasts from throughout the area. The Savannah Hockey Classic pits college club teams against each other, vying for the coveted Thrasher Cup. Old rivalries simmer anew when Georgia faces Georgia Tech and Florida skates against Florida State. Day two sees the teams trade up, squaring off against their varsity conference foes. Bring the kids for the fun and games, and stick around for autograph sessions after each matchup. The Civic Center concessions serve beer to the adult crowd, and the Classic has become a favorite starting spot for evenings out on the town. No, it may not be the familiar gridiron Southern sports fans are used to, but it doesn't take long for this rumble in the rink to create new hockey fans.

savannahhockeyclassic.com

DRIFT THROUGH
THE AREA'S NATURAL HISTORY

The Intracoastal Waterway divides Georgia's coast into a series of barrier islands. Winding between these islands are calm waterways, abutted on either side by scenic marshes and thriving wildlife habitats. Inaccessible by car or even by foot, the only way to see this part of the Savannah area is to take to the water. Fortunately, several local companies offer options for a waterway outing, including a pair of popular guided kayak tours. Savannah Canoe and Kayak will take you to any one of a half-dozen breathtaking spots, including the historic Cockspur Lighthouse and the Salt Creek Trails of uninhabited Little Tybee Island. Moon River Kayak Tours takes guests through the tranquil waters of its namesake river and the narrows near Skidaway Island. Keep an eye out for majestic eagles and osprey, and if you're lucky, our local dolphins might pay you a visit, too.

Savannah Canoe and Kayak
savannahcanoeandkayak.com

Moon River Kayak Tours
moonriverkayak.com

PEDAL THE STREETS
AFTER DARK

Savannah is known as a walkable city, and one group wants to make it a bike-able city, as well. The Savannah Bicycle Campaign encourages locals to use two wheels on their daily commute, and they promote this mission through the Midnight Garden Ride, their annual fall event. Gathering more than 500 riders, the police-escorted bike ride weaves through some of Savannah's most beautiful neighborhoods, offering a unique evening view of the city's homes and architecture. In addition to being a tour, the ride is also a celebration. Designated cyclists pump upbeat tunes from portable speakers, and costumes are strongly encouraged for all riders. The 7 p.m. start encourages full-family participation, though the beer flows freely at the afterparty for any grown-up riders craving something more than the contents of their water bottles.

midnightgardenride.com

CULTURE AND HISTORY

GET CULTURED
WITH THREE CENTURIES OF ART

Opened in 1886, Telfair Museums is the oldest public art museum in the South, one of the first ten art museums in America, and the very first founded by a woman, Mary Telfair. The original site, Telfair Academy, once served as a mansion at the center of Savannah's high society. Two of the rooms are preserved true to their nineteenth century splendor, while the rest of the Academy showcases some of the museum's most popular and enduring works from the nineteenth and twentieth centuries. If contemporary art is more your thing, jaunt across the street to the sleek and modern Jepson Center, designed by world-renowned architect Moshe Safdie and opened in 2006. A sweeping staircase leads you straight from Telfair Square up to the main galleries, where you'll find a mix of Telfair favorites alongside traveling exhibitions. Don't miss the iconic *Bird Girl* statue, made famous on the cover of *Midnight in the Garden of Good and Evil*.

121 Barnard St., 912-790-8800
telfair.org

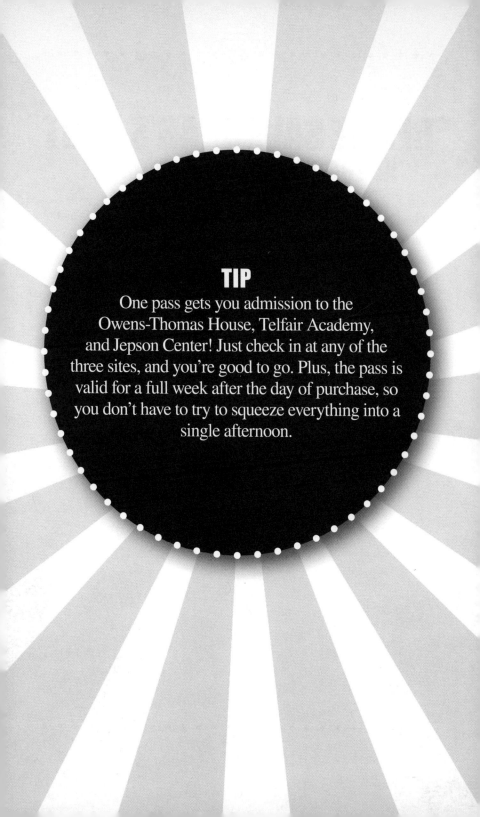

TIP

One pass gets you admission to the Owens-Thomas House, Telfair Academy, and Jepson Center! Just check in at any of the three sites, and you're good to go. Plus, the pass is valid for a full week after the day of purchase, so you don't have to try to squeeze everything into a single afternoon.

RELIVE SAVANNAH'S PAST
AT THE OWENS-THOMAS HOUSE

In a city filled with historic homes, there is none as popular as the stately Owens-Thomas House on Oglethorpe Square. Designed by the young, gallivanting English architect William Jay and completed in 1819, the mansion is heralded as one of the finest examples of Regency-style architecture in America. Professional guides lead each forty-five minute tour, covering the story of the families who called the mansion home, Savannah's history in general, and Jay's signature architectural style. The tour includes one of the only intact urban slave quarters in America, complete with the original haint blue paint used to ward off evil spirits. An intricate rain collection and cistern system made the home one of America's first with indoor plumbing, preceding even the White House.

124 Abercorn St., 912-790-8800
telfair.org/owens-thomas

LEARN THE STORY
OF CIVIL RIGHTS IN SAVANNAH

While Savannah isn't the first place mentioned in regards to America's Civil Rights movement, the city produced many prominent activists, notably Wesley W. Law, Hosea Williams, and Mayor Malcolm MacLean. Perhaps most notable of all was Dr. Ralph M. Gilbert, a minister at Savannah's historic First African Baptist Church and a leader in the NAACP. Today, his legacy is commemorated at the Ralph Mark Gilbert Civil Rights Museum on Martin Luther King Jr. Boulevard. The museum resides in the building of the old Wage Earners Savings and Loan Bank, which operated as the county's largest bank serving African Americans. Three floors are filled with photographic and interactive exhibits, presenting the history of Civil Rights in Savannah and celebrating the people who strove to make our city a more equitable place to live.

460 MLK Jr. Blvd., 912-777-6099
visit-historic-savannah.com/ralph-mark-gilbert-civil-rights-museum.html

DON YOUR BRIGHTEST
GREEN GARB

Savannah's iconic St. Patrick's Day Parade traces its roots back to the early 1800s. Today, the celebration ranks as one of the largest in the world, swelling the population of the Historic District ten times over every year on March 17. Hundreds of thousands of people line the parade route, and locals know to set up tents and chairs starting early in the morning, turning the city's squares into one giant party. After the parade, the official party starts in City Market and on River Street, where the raucous—and drunken—festivities ensue full force. The parade itself, though, is always family-friendly, featuring bands, fun floats, a dozen Shriner units, and more Savannah-Irish clans than you can shake a shillelagh at.

savannahsaintpatricksday.com

TIP

Parking comes at a premium on parade day, so plan to arrive early. There are also park-and-ride options from locations outside of the parade zone, and if you're willing to walk, parking even a mile to the south of the parade route can save you the headache of searching for a space. If you party hard, a host of taxis, Ubers, Lyfts, and even bicycle cabs are available to get you back home or to a hotel, safe and sound.

A SAVANNAH STORY
FIT FOR A NOVEL

Flannery O'Connor once wrote: "Anybody who has survived his childhood has enough information about life to last him the rest of his days." Regarded as one of the most important writers of the twentieth century, O'Connor was born in Savannah and spent the first part of her childhood in a home on Lafayette Square. Today, that home operates as a museum celebrating Flannery's legacy, with a special emphasis on her local ties. Docent-led tours share the story of a precocious young Flannery and reveal the Savannah roots that anchor so much of her writing, including the tale of her famous backward-walking chicken. The home also presents two annual lecture series featuring regional writers and scholars and a Flannery birthday party and parade, as well as several other marquee events throughout the year.

207 E. Charlton St., 912-233-6014
flanneryoconnorhome.org

FORTIFY YOURSELF
FOR A PIECE OF CIVIL WAR HISTORY

Today, Fort Pulaski presents a grand, imposing face to visitors, but its walls still bear the scars of the Civil War. A coastal fortification completed in the mid-nineteenth century, the fort is named in honor of Revolutionary War hero Casimir Pulaski, who died following wounds sustained in a battle to retake Savannah. Claimed by Confederate soldiers at the start of the Civil War, the fort eventually fell to Union forces, who used the new technology of rifled cannon barrels to render the brick and mortar walls useless. Tour the fort itself (forty-five-minute guided tours are offered throughout the day), and leave time for a casual hike along one of several scenic trails. History buffs and nature lovers alike should find a peaceful afternoon in a truly stunning setting.

U.S. 80 (Tybee Rd.), 912-786-5787
nps.gov/fopu

LOOK UP FOR
DIVERSE ARCHITECTURE

Almost 300 years of architectural styles surround the Historic District's green-filled squares. To stroll the streets is to immerse yourself in a living architectural laboratory. Homes from the eighteenth century stand next to twentieth-century structures, and somehow it all fits into a seamless whole. While the city is beautiful enough for the casual visitor, if you're looking for a deeper understanding of how it all came together, try Architectural Tours of Savannah. Founder Jonathan Stalcup takes guests on comprehensive walking tours of Savannah's finest buildings and shares how the Historic District grew from Colonial homesteads and stately mansions into a modern cityscape. A trained architect, Stalcup combines his professional knowledge with a flair for storytelling, providing a tour that appeals to architectural experts and novices alike.

912-604-6354
architecturalsavannah.com

SNAP A SELFIE
AT THE FORSYTH PARK FOUNTAIN

Savannah is filled with scenic backdrops, but the fountain in Forsyth Park finds its way into photos more often than any other spot in the city. Forsyth claims thirty acres at the south end of the Historic District, making it the largest greenspace in the Downtown area. In warm weather, the open fields play host to sunbathers and pick-up games of football, soccer, and Frisbee. The tree-filled northern half of the park provides shady spots and plenty of benches for a breather after a long day of walking the city. Forsyth also serves as home to many of Savannah's festivals and special events, including Picnic in the Park, Savannah Pride Festival, SCAD's Sidewalk Arts Festival, plus too many more to name. Stop by any Saturday morning for the only farmers' market Downtown. And don't forget to strike a pose in front of the fountain before you leave.

Bull St., between Gaston St. and Park St.

STAY UP TO DATE WITH
CONTEMPORARY ART

The Savannah College of Art and Design welcomes around 8,000 students to Savannah each year. This influx of creative talent has played a large part in turning Savannah into the artistic hub of the region. To serve its students, as well as Savannah residents and visitors, the university expanded the SCAD Museum of Art in 2011, installing new galleries in the shell of an old railroad warehouse. The stunning building, designed in part by SCAD faculty, can claim to be a work of art in and of itself. It houses a rotating schedule of cutting-edge contemporary and modern art, drawing from SCAD's own considerable holdings as well as bringing in the work of artists from across the nation. Check the website to see what's on view when you plan to visit.

601 Turner Blvd., 912-525-7191
scadmoa.org

TRAVEL TO
SAVANNAH'S PAST

The moment you pass through the front gates of Wormsloe, you're transported to another world. Ancient oak trees on either side of the main drive form natural arches, a leafy tunnel stretching for hundreds of yards. The drive leads into the heart of the Colonial estate of Noble Jones, one of Georgia's earliest settlers—he arrived with Georgia founder James Edward Oglethorpe on the first boat. Park at Wormsloe's small history museum, and then be prepared to walk. Well-marked trails guide visitors to important sites around the property, and you're likely to encounter historic reenactors demonstrating the Colonial lifestyle. The trails lead through moss-draped forest and run alongside scenic views of the marsh. And make sure to scout out the tabby ruins of Jones's estate, the oldest extant structure in all of Georgia.

7601 Skidaway Rd., 912-353-3023
gastateparks.org/wormsloe

PAY YOUR RESPECTS TO
SAVANNAH'S HISTORY

A city like Savannah has seen its fair share of famous residents, and places like Downtown's Colonial Cemetery are chock full of historical markers. But it's the sprawling Bonaventure Cemetery, tucked between the unassuming town of Thunderbolt and the Wilmington River, where you can discover the perfect mix of Savannah's history and its beauty. The 160-acre sanctuary rose to fame in part due to Jack Leigh's iconic Bird Girl photograph on the cover of *Midnight in the Garden of Good and Evil* (the *Bird Girl* statue featured in the photograph has since been moved to Telfair Museums' Jepson Center). Even before "the book," Bonaventure was visited for its monuments, grand old oaks, and views over the Intracoastal Waterway. Search out the graves of songwriter Johnny Mercer, poet Conrad Aiken, and even Jack Leigh himself.

330 Bonaventure Rd., Thunderbolt
bonaventurehistorical.org

CLIMB TO THE TOP
OF TYBEE ISLAND

Most people head to Tybee Island for a day in the sun or an evening in one of the town's idiosyncratic bars. The island boasts a rich history, however, and the Tybee Lighthouse is one of the area's most recognizable landmarks. The current lighthouse is the third-and-a-half built on Tybee to guide ships safely into the Savannah River channel. The lower half of the current structure dates to 1773, while the upper portion was rebuilt following the Civil War. The lighthouse's legacy shines all the way back to the earliest years of the colony, when Georgia's founder ordered construction of lighthouse number one. Today, visitors can take the 178 steps to the top for a view out over the Atlantic and back toward the mainland. Admission includes a stop in the Tybee Museum, housed in the old Fort Screven battery.

30 Meddin Dr., Tybee Island, 912-786-5801
tybeelighthouse.org

CHALK IT UP FOR ART

Savannah College of Art and Design hosts several marquee events throughout the year, but none are as popular as the Sidewalk Arts Festival. The Forsyth Park–based event has ushered in the spring season for more than thirty-five years and has grown into an all-day extravaganza, featuring hundreds of SCAD students and alumni creating a staggering array of chalk artwork on the park's sidewalks. Each artist is assigned a section of sidewalk, and they hunch over those small plots for hours, chalking everything from portraits to cartoons to abstract art. While plenty of participants are simply focused on having fun, prizes are awarded in several categories, and the best creations would be worthy of inclusion in a museum. Come early to see works in progress or in the afternoon to behold the finished masterpieces. Plus, there's live music, food, and activities all day long for the whole family.

scad.edu/sidewalkarts

TOUR THE HISTORIC HOME
THAT STARTED IT ALL

The story of the Davenport House is the story of historic preservation in Savannah. Originally built in 1820, the house faced demolition in the mid-twentieth century. Fortunately, local activists formed the Savannah Historic Foundation in 1955 to save the Davenport House, which would become the first of hundreds of historic buildings preserved by the organization. The house itself represents a simple take on late Federalist-style architecture, and the interior has been restored to its appearance as of 1827, the year the home's original owner, Isaiah Davenport, died. The Savannah Historic Foundation continues to operate the Davenport House as a museum, offering guided tours seven days a week. A team of knowledgeable docents leads guests through all three floors, sharing tales from the home's past and its place in Savannah history.

324 E. State St., 912-236-8097
davenporthousemuseum.org

SET SAIL
FOR THE HISTORY
OF AMERICAN SEAFARING

As a port city, Savannah has been tied to the sea since the day it was founded, and you can discover the city's whole nautical history at Ships of the Sea Maritime Museum. The museum's collection includes nautical-themed art, artifacts, and nine galleries full of intricately detailed ship models, from local namesakes Steamship Savannah and City of Savannah to the Titanic and a whole fleet of modern naval vessels. Fans of architecture will love the museum building itself, the historic Scarbrough House, which was built in 1819 by British architect William Jay (Jay also designed the Owens-Thomas House and Telfair Academy). If you have little ones in tow, know that the models are kept safely behind glass, so Ships of the Sea makes a great place to keep curious kids engaged for a whole afternoon.

41 MLK Jr. Blvd., 912-232-1511
shipsofthesea.org

TIP

Get a historic bang for your buck with the Pioneers in Preservation Triple Pass, which grants you access to the Davenport House, Andrew Low House, and Ships of the Sea Museum all for one discounted price. Purchase a pass online from the Historic Savannah Foundation or in person at any of the three sites.

myhsf.org

SCOUT OUT A PIECE
OF NATIONAL HISTORY

Walking through Downtown, you might think that Savannah is home to more Girl Scouts per capita than anywhere else in the nation. Daisies and Brownies abound, and you're likely to pass a procession of sash-clad Scouts anywhere you walk. But few of those groups call Savannah home. The Girl Scouts as an organization, however, can trace its roots right back to the heart of the city. Founder Juliette Gordon Low was born and died in Savannah and founded America's first troop here in 1912. Her birthplace is now a public house museum and serves as a hub for visiting Scouts. In addition, her adult home, the Andrew Low House, is also open to the public, as well as the carriage house out back, where the Girl Scouts made their first headquarters in America.

Juliette Gordon Low Birthplace
10 E. Oglethorpe Ave., 912-233-4501
juliettegordonlowbirthplace.org

Andrew Low House
329 Abercorn St., 912-233-6854
andrewlowhouse.com

HOP A RIDE
TO SEE ALL OF SAVANNAH'S SIGHTS

Today, you can choose from several quality trolley tours in Savannah, but once upon a time there was only one. That company, Old Savannah Tours, is still around today and is still owned and operated by locals. There's also the local branch of national sightseeing chain Old Town Trolley. Both operate trolley-style buses that run on a continuous loop through the Historic District, offering general and specialized tours. If you're short on time, take Old Savannah's ninety minute overview tour. If you want to check out individual attractions along the way, both companies offer on/off passes, so you can hitch a ride on any trolley that comes by. Old Savannah also brings history to life with a rotating cast of characters along the route, from pirates to prominent Georgians and even Forrest Gump.

Old Savannah Tours
250 MLK Jr. Blvd., 800-517-9007
oldsavannahtours.com

Old Town Trolley
855-245-8992
trolleytours.com/savannah

DISCOVER SAVANNAH'S
RICH AFRICAN AMERICAN HISTORY

Built shortly after Emancipation, the Beach Institute became Savannah's first school for African Americans, educating thousands of students until it was replaced by newer schools in 1919. Today, the King-Tisdell Cottage Foundation, founded by legendary Civil Rights leader W.W. Law, operates the original structure as a cultural center and museum, with four floors open to the public. Permanent history installations are supplemented by a rotating selection of exhibitions by African American artists from the South and beyond, including one of the nation's finest collections of wood carvings by renowned Savannah folk artist Ulysses Davis. In addition to its galleries, the Institute maintains several event spaces and hosts lectures, concerts, and other performances throughout the year.

502 E. Harris St., 912-335-8868
beachinstitute.org

TOUR THE HOUSE
THAT PUT SAVANNAH ON THE MAP

The Mercer-Williams House rose to fame—or infamy—as the home of Jim Williams, the central figure in John Berendt's bestselling book *Midnight in the Garden of Good and Evil*. It was in this house that Williams killed his personal assistant, setting off a string of trials that brought the then-sleepy Southern town of Savannah into the national spotlight. But the house's history extends all the way back to the Civil War, when General Hugh W. Mercer (great-grandfather of songwriter Johnny Mercer) began construction, which was completed by the home's first resident, John Wilder. Williams acquired the house in 1969 and filled it with extravagant furnishings, many of which are still on view. Guided tours are offered daily, and the Carriage House Gift Shop is one of the best places to find a Savannah souvenir.

429 Bull St., 912-236-6352
mercerhouse.com

GET SCHOOLED
IN LOCAL HISTORY

The Massie Heritage Center opened its doors in 1856 as the first public school in Savannah. Today, it has been converted into a museum and education center and presents a comprehensive introduction to the city. Tour Massie's exhibits for an overview of local history and culture, including fun installations geared to educate and entertain kids of all ages. Find period costumes, a fully furnished nineteenth century classroom, and a scale model of the entire Historic District. Massie also offers a great introduction to local architecture, with a focus on the classical details found on the city's most magnificent buildings. Massie itself was designed in the Greek Revival style, and though a single building, the wings were designed to look like separate structures to better blend in with the adjacent townhomes on Calhoun Square.

207 E. Gordon St., 912-395-5070
savannah.chatham.k12.ga.us/schools/massie

EXPLORE SAVANNAH'S
WILD SIDE

If you grew up in Savannah, chances are you have fond memories of grade school field trips to the Oatland Island Wildlife Center. Oatland has educated area students for generations and also welcomes general visitors seven days a week. More than 150 animals call the center home, thriving in large natural habitats spread out across the island. Stroll among the habitats on rustic trails that weave through preserved woods and marshes. While not a zoo in the traditional sense, there are plenty of highlights for the animal lover in your party. Glimpse a cougar or bobcat. Get up close to bison or deer. Look up for birds of prey. Reptiles are represented by gators and a gopher tortoise. And the youngest members of your party will love the kid-friendly barnyard.

711 Sandtown Rd., 912-395-1212
savannah.chatham.k12.ga.us/schools/oat

MAKE CONTACT
WITH SAVANNAH'S OTHER SIDE

A city as old as Savannah is bound to have a few ghosts, and there are tour guides aplenty willing to tell you tales of the supernatural. A few favorite options include Blue Orb Tours, offering both adult and family-friendly options; Ghost City Tours, featuring spirits of both the ethereal and liquid variety on its Haunted Pub Crawl; and Hearse Ghost Tours, in which you ride around in—you guessed it—a converted hearse. Some tours even provide after-hours access to favorite Savannah historic sites, as well as stories not told by the daytime docents. Hear one of the several theories behind the haunting of the Sorrel-Weed House. Learn the tragic tale of Anne Powers, who still supposedly resides in room 204 at the 1790 Inn, long after her death. Is it fact or is it fiction? No one can say, but whichever tour you choose, be prepared to be scared.

Blue Orb Tours
912-665-4258
blueorbtours.com

Ghost City Tours
888-859-5375
ghosttoursinsavannah.com

Hearse Ghost Tours
912-695-1578
hearseghosttours.com

TOUR SAVANNAH'S
MAJESTIC CATHEDRAL

The Catholic Church established the Diocese of Savannah in 1850, making the city the hub of religious life for thousands of Georgia and Florida residents. To reflect the city's new stature, and to accommodate a growing Catholic population, the Cathedral of St. John the Baptist was completed in 1876. Originally a brick structure in the French Gothic style, spires were added and the bricks stuccoed not long after construction. A fire destroyed all but the exterior walls in 1898, however, and it would not be until the new century that the building finally reopened. Interior renovations continued for a decade more, including sweeping murals and stained glass, completing the grand sanctuary that visitors see today. Self-guided tours are encouraged Monday through Saturday, as long as no worship service is in progress.

222 E. Harris St., 912-233-4709
savannahcathedral.org

MAKE YOURSELF AT HOME
IN SAVANNAH'S FINEST HOUSES

Stately mansions overlook most of Savannah's squares, and elegant townhomes line the streets throughout the Historic and Victorian districts. For every home that's been turned into a museum, there are dozens that remain private residences. You can always take in the exteriors, of course, but for one spring weekend each year, private owners swing open their doors for the Savannah Tour of Homes and Gardens. See treasured furnishings that have been passed down through generations of Savannahians and step into the beautiful greenspaces of walled gardens. The event has grown to include several different walking tours in different regions of the city, as well as lectures and fine dining experiences. Purchase admission for individual events, or take it all in with a combo ticket.

savannahtourofhomes.org

CELEBRATE THE CITY'S
DIVERSE HERITAGE

The Hostess City prides itself on welcoming all visitors. Over the centuries, people from across the globe have accepted that warm welcome and decided to stick around. Today, the various cultures that make up Savannah celebrate their heritages in a vibrant series of annual festivals. The Savannah Irish Festival kicks off the St. Patrick's Day season (yes, it's a whole season here) with two days of live music, performances, and general socializing. The Savannah Black Heritage Festival offers an extensive schedule of lectures and performances for the whole of Black History Month. Savannah's foodies never miss the Shalom Y'all Food Fest hosted by Congregation Mickve Israel. The Savannah Greek Festival and Asian Cultural Festival serve up equal portions of traditional fare and culture. These festivals welcome all comers, so there's no better place to get to know your neighbors.

Savannah Irish Festival
savannahirish.org

Savannah Black Heritage Festival
savannahblackheritagefestival.com

Shalom Y'all Food Fest
mickveisrael.org/food-fest

Savannah Greek Festival
savannahgreekfest.com

Savannah Asian Cultural Festival
armstrong.edu/about/savannah-asian-cultural-festival

A FAMILY TRIP
THROUGH SAVANNAH'S PAST

Located adjacent to the Downtown Visitors Information Center, Tricentennial Park has emerged as a favorite destination for families. The park comprises three separate venues: the Georgia State Railroad Museum, Savannah History Museum, and Savannah Children's Museum. Kids love climbing aboard the big engines at the Railroad Museum, and check the schedule for daily rides on historic trains. Plus, the old turntable is still fully functional. Keep the tykes busy at the outdoor Children's Museum, a recent addition to the park, but already one of the city's top spots for hands-on, family-friendly fun. Lastly, learn the whole story of Savannah's past, from the American Revolution through the Civil War and beyond, at the History Museum. Cap off your visit with a walk across the street to Battlefield Memorial Park, site of one of the Revolutionary War's fiercest battles.

303 MLK Jr. Blvd., 912-651-6825
chsgeorgia.org/tcp

VISIT SAVANNAH'S
ORIGINAL TOURIST DESTINATION

For generations, no place in Savannah has drawn as many tourists as River Street. The buildings that line the base of Yamacraw Bluff date back more than a century, and the river walk extends from one end of the Historic District to the other. Once cotton warehouses, the whole strip has been converted into shops, restaurants, bars, and hotels. Stroll along the Savannah River during the day, stopping for lunch at decades-old standards such as Spanky's or the Exchange. Stick around for late-night carousing and get a cup of the "coldest, cheapest beer in town" from the Warehouse. Don't forget that you can take the drink with you to enjoy waterside. River Street also hosts some of the city's premier events, from art festivals to pub crawls, as well as fireworks shows on the Fouth of July, New Year's, and the first Friday of every month.

riverstreetsavannah.com

HANDS-ON HISTORY

What was that bang? Probably one of the daily cannon firings at Old Fort Jackson, a National Historic Landmark just a few minutes' drive from Downtown. Constructed in the early nineteenth century, the fort played an important role during the Civil War, first as a last line of defense for the Confederate-controlled port, and then as a garrison for Union troops after Sherman took Savannah. The fort is now Georgia's oldest standing brick fortification and operates as a favorite site for local field trips and families looking for a slice of history beyond the Historic District. Interactive programs introduce visitors to the site's storied past and are perfect for engaging the kids. Make sure you plan your visit to catch a cannon firing up close. They light the fuse at 11 a.m. and 2 p.m., though they recommend that you call ahead to confirm the daily schedule.

1 Fort Jackson Rd., 912-232-3945
chsgeorgia.org/OFJ

SEE THE WHOLE
HISTORIC DISTRICT ON A SINGLE STROLL

Savannah claims to be one of the most walkable cities in the world, and you can make it from one end of the Historic District to another in a matter of minutes. Choose a path through Savannah's historic squares, tree-filled parks intersected by the main north/south thoroughfares. In the squares you'll find everything from monuments and historical markers to gazebos and the remains of an old cistern system. If the north end of Chippewa Square looks familiar, that's where Tom Hanks waited for his bus in *Forrest Gump*. The square also features a bold statue of Georgia's founder, James Edward Oglethorpe. Just a block away in Wright Square, Tomochichi's rock commemorates the Native American leader who gave Oglethorpe the land on which Savannah now stands. Wherever you walk, make sure to look up. The old oaks and diverse architecture make every square unique.

Photo credit: Cohen's Retreat Brown Dog Market

SHOPPING AND FASHION

STROLL THE DOWNTOWN
SHOPPING DISTRICT

Awesome shops dot the Historic District, but you can find the highest concentration on Broughton Street, which features national chains alongside Savannah stalwarts. Local jeweler Zia sells his own delicate wares, plus a selection of bold accent pieces, from a corner shop on the west end. The Paris Market stocks two floors with Continental ecclectables. Civvies puts the hip in hipster with only the coolest second-hand clothes and accessories. J. Parker has helped define the look of Savannah's gentlemen for more than forty years. And find your geek fix at Planet Fun, a vintage toy and comic shop that caters to the kid in all of us. You'll have no trouble filling your whole afternoon—not to mention several shopping bags—without ever turning off the main drag.

Zia Jewelry + Accessories
325 W. Broughton St., 912-233-3237
ziaboutique.com

Paris Market
36 W. Broughton St., 912-232-1500
theparismarket.com

Civvies New & Recycled Clothing
14 E. Broughton St., 912-236-1551
civviesclothes.com

J. Parker Ltd.
20 W. Broughton St., 912-234-0004
jparkerltd.com

Planet Fun
127 E. Broughton St., 912-201-0228
facebook.com/planetfuntoys

SPRUCE UP YOUR SPACE
AT 24E

24e Design Co. claims to be the city's coolest shop, and most patrons agree. Owned by a Savannah native, 24e collects home furnishings from the world over, plus a selection of homegrown originals. Browse high-end furniture fit for a Manhattan loft, from chic seating to bold lamps to tables made from old bowling lanes. Check out exclusive designs crafted from reclaimed airplane parts, including coffee tables, end tables, and desks. 24e even carries a free-standing aluminum bar fashioned from an airplane fuselage. On any given day in the shop, you might find a handmade foosball table, a swinging couch hanging from the ceiling, or vintage artillery shells turned into works of art. Since you can't very well fit a sofa into your carry-on luggage, 24e also curates a selection of bag-friendly gift items.

24 E. Broughton St., 912-233-2274
24estyle.com

STOCK UP ON
LOCAL ART

The Savannah College of Art and Design has been turning out talented artists for decades, and while most of them leave Savannah after graduation, you can still find their best work at shopSCAD. The university-run store occupies a corner of the original SCAD building, Poetter Hall, on Madison Square. Creative window displays catch the eyes of passersby, and more art awaits inside. Contemporary paintings, prints, and photographs dominate one wall, and there are additional art racks in the back of the shop. SCAD also offers programs in fields such as fashion and fibers, so the shop carries hand-made accessories, cutting-edge jewelry, and unique home furnishings. Remember, everything in the store was made by SCAD students, alumni, and faculty, so you can take home an exclusive piece of Savannah's creative spirit.

340 Bull St., 912-525-5180
shopscad.com

FIND A SOUVENIR
WORTH SAVORING

There may be no more popular Savannah souvenir than a jar of honey from Savannah Bee Company. Locally owned and operated since 2002, the company claims to produce the finest honey *in the world*. Stop in its flagship Broughton Street location, and step up to the honey bar for free samples of the most popular products. The store itself is worth a tour, a mix of rustic wood and glowing, golden jars, staffed by friendly and expert honey-lovers. Savannah Bee's products aren't limited to just the sweet stuff, either. The shop sells its own line of health and beauty items, bee-themed gifts, plus all the accessories you need to enjoy honey like a professional beekeeper.

104 W. Broughton St., 912-233-7873
savannahbee.com

TIP

For the twenty-one-and-up crowd, take a seat at the Mead Bar in the back of the store for a tasting of several fine honey wines.

SAY HELLO TO
THE BOOK LADY

After a long day of touring the sites of Savannah, sometimes the best thing is to kick back in a local coffee shop with a good book. Don't worry if you forgot to pack one, though, because the Book Lady Bookstore has you covered. Tucked into a garden-level space on Liberty Street, the Book Lady's shelves are stuffed with a quality selection of new and used books in all genres. Claim the store's sofa to read a few pages before you buy, and don't miss the small room in the back, where you'll find paperback literary fiction and a table of staff favorites. The Book Lady also hosts regular literary events and readings, so keep an eye out for favorite local and touring authors making appearances in the intimate space.

6 E. Liberty St., 912-233-3628
thebookladybookstore.com

SHOP LIKE A BOHEMIAN

Much of the Savannah experience is packed into the Historic District, but if you're willing to trek a couple miles south on Bull Street, you'll come to the resurgent Starland District. The district is named after the former Starland Dairy, which sits at its center. The original dairy buildings have been repurposed as posh condos and trendy storefronts, housing eclectic shops featuring local arts and crafts, clothing, accessories, and consignment. The Wormhole has anchored the district's music scene for years, and the Starland Cafe has served great grub since before the area was cool. Starlandia Creative Supply accepts leftover art supplies from departing SCAD students, reselling them at a huge discount. Several favorite Savannah eateries also call the district home, including Back in the Day Bakery, so plan your visit around mealtime.

The Wormhole
2307 Bull St., 912-713-2855
wormholebar.com

Starlandia Creative Supply
2438 Bull St., 912-417-4561
starlandiasupply.com

Starland Cafe
114 E 41st St., 912-433-9355
starlanddining.com

Back in the Day Bakery
2403 Bull St., 912-495-9292
backinthedaybakery.com

starlanddistrict.com

STOCK YOUR
BOOKSHELVES AT E. SHAVER

Readers, rejoice! Savannah's other iconic bookstore is less than a block away from the Book Lady. E. Shaver opened her namesake bookstore in 1975, making it the oldest in the city, and stocked its shelves with a comprehensive collection of classic literature and new releases. Shaver's successor has maintained the store's charm while increasing its focus on fine contemporary writing. The new releases section contains a veritable who's who of today's best fiction and nonfiction writers. Look to your right when you walk in the door for an extensive selection of Savannah- and Southern-themed books. E. Shaver also sponsors several reading groups and book clubs, which meet in the shop's back room. And check its calendar for readings and book signings by writers touring the region.

326 Bull St., 912-234-7257
eshaverbooks.com

GALLERY HOP
WITH ONLY ONE STOP

The Starland District's Sulfur Studios opened only a few short years ago, but it's already staked a claim at the center of Savannah's art world. Occupying an old two-story commercial complex, Sulfur is jam-packed with artists' studios in what were once meeting rooms and offices. Individual artists and collectives use these spaces as both working studios and storefronts, and Sulfur has public hours on weekends plus one evening a month during First Fridays in Starland. Artists sell everything from fine art to jewelry to lapel pins, and much of their work can't be found anywhere else. Sulfur's main art gallery has become one of the city's most popular exhibition and event spaces, so check its calendar to see upcoming offerings, including solo and group art shows, performances, and community gatherings.

2301 Bull St., 912-231-7105
sulfurstudios.org

GIVE A GIFT
TO YOUR CREATIVE SIDE

Twenty years ago, no one would have given a single thought to Cohen's Retreat as a shopping destination. That's because back then Cohen's served as a care facility for elderly men, many of whom you could find sitting on benches by Skidaway Road, waving to passing cars. While the old men may have moved on, their friendly spirit remains, and today the Retreat runs as a center for creative enterprises. Design-based businesses occupy offices upstairs, and individual artists rent studios and bungalows on the premises. There's even a gourmet restaurant. But shoppers will delight most in the south wing, the Brown Dog Market, a series of curated showrooms stocked with wares by local, regional, and national artists and artisans. Browse home goods, one-of-a-kind fashions, decorations, and more! And know that your purchase supports the local creative community.

5715 Skidaway Rd., 912-355-3336
cohensretreat.com

ART EXCLUSIVE
TO SAVANNAH

Savannah's historic City Market might best be known today as a spot for outdoor music and late night barhopping, but during the daylight hours you can get your fill of shopping, too. Several gift shops occupy the street-level storefronts, perfect for finding collectibles and keepsakes. Continue down the strip for shops offering accessories, clothing, and jewelry, ranging from fun to fancy. And speaking of jewels, the crowning glory of City Market can be found in the upstairs art galleries. The second floor of the whole west half of the market is divided into studio spaces for individual artists. Catch them plying their trades, including everything from painting and sculpture to photography and folk art. Much of the art can only be found in Savannah, so you can take home a souvenir that's an authentic piece of local culture.

savannahcitymarket.com

TAKE HOME A PIECE
OF HISTORY

Feeling inspired by your historic surroundings? Claim a piece of that history for your own home at one of Savannah's numerous antique shops. Jere's Antiques has been selling fine furnishings since 1976. Discover eighteenth, nineteenth, and twentieth-century treasures on a stroll through its huge downtown warehouse. Head over to Bull Street for Southern Charm Antiques, which curates a lavish mix of antique wares in a cozy storefront. A little further up Bull, George Davis Antiques specializes in pre-1900 European furniture. And just before you reach Forsyth Park, Alex Raskin Antiques stuffs the historic Noble Hardee Mansion with wall-to-wall wares. Beyond these mainstays, keep an eye out for smaller shops specializing in everything from antique books to vintage maps.

Jere's Antiques
9 N. Jefferson St., 912-236-2815
jeresantiques.com

George Davis Antiques
408 Bull St., 912-232-6603
facebook.com/George-Davis-Antiques-Interiors-111017425592191/

Southern Charm Antiques
250 Bull St., 912-233-9797
southerncharmantiques.com

Alex Raskin Antiques
441 Bull St., 912-232-8205
alexraskinantiques.com

GIVE YOUR HOME
A FABULOUS FLOURISH

If you describe your decor as "eclectic" or "funky," then Two Women and a Warehouse likely stocks what you're looking for. This Midtown staple hosts twenty unique vendors in a 7,000-square-foot warehouse off Bull Street, just a few hundred yards south of the Starland District. The Warehouse specializes in reclaimed furniture, refurbished and painted in catchy colors. Chests, armoires, desks, and chairs abound, as well as off-the-wall finds such as library carts and antique school desks. In addition to furniture, browse original arts and crafts, knickknacks, and a slew of artifacts representing the best of twentieth-century Americana. With reasonable prices for truly individual pieces, the Warehouse has become a favorite shop for young professionals and college students, as well as the arts and crafts crowd.

2819 Bull St., 912-351-5040
twowomenandawarehouse.com

SNACK ON THE ORIGINAL
SAVANNAH TREAT

Since 1924, Byrd Cookie Company has been baking batches of Savannah's favorite sweet treats. Today, you can find Byrd's cookies in shops around the Historic District, as well as in four dedicated Byrd stores. The flagship store on Waters Avenue also houses the bakery, and you can smell the delicious aroma of fresh cookies as soon as you step inside. The store sells its whole line of crispy, bite-sized cookies, from classic flavors like the Key Lime Coolers and Cheddar Pecan Biscuits to the one-of-a-kind Georgia Peach Cookie. Byrd's treats come in a variety of gift packs and collectible tins featuring iconic Savannah scenes, so they make perfectly packable gifts to take to family and friends back home.

6700 Waters Ave., 912-721-1526
byrdcookiecompany.com

SUGGESTED
ITINERARIES

A LANDSCAPE FOR ART LOVERS

A LOOK BACK FOR HISTORY BUFFS

BRING THE WHOLE FAMILY

STAY STYLISH

TOP NOSH

CHEERS!

LISTEN UP

THE GREAT OUTDOORS

ACTIVITIES
BY SEASON

WINTER

Plug In for PULSE, 52

Heat Up the Rink, 69

SPRING

Cross the Savannah River on Foot, 67

Chalk It Up for Art, 88

Don Your Brightest Green Garb, 78

Make Yourself at Home in Savannah's Finest Houses, 101

SUMMER

Savannah Goes Bananas for Baseball, 64

Dip Your Toes in the Atlantic, 65

FALL

Pace Yourself for the Big Race, 68

Taste All of Savannah's Best Bites at One Event, 26

Pedal the Streets after Dark, 71

INDEX

Photo credit: Geoff Johnson